W9-CJZ-549

AFTER THE STRAVINSKY CONCERT
And Other Poems

AFTER THE
STRAVINSKY CONCERT

And Other Poems.

CONSTANCE HUNTING

MIDDLEBURY COLLEGE LIBRARY.

Charles Scribner's Sons ✿ New York

PS
3558
U5
A68

3/1981
Senl

Copyright © 1969 Constance Hunting

The following poems appeared first in the magazines indicated below:

The Christian Century (October 13, 1965 issue)
"Conversation: Late Day."
Copyright 1965 Christian Century Foundation. Reprinted by permission.
Fiddlehead (Spring 1964)
"Revenant."
The Massachusetts Review (Autumn 1961, Volume III, No. 1)
"Miss Dickinson."
Copyright © 1961 The Massachusetts Review, Inc.
Poetry (September 1960 issue)
"After the Stravinsky Concert," "Afternoon of a Contemporary Poet," and "A Dream of Heavenly Love and Redemption in the Wood." Copyright © 1960 Constance Hunting and Modern Poetry Association.
The Sparrow Magazine (April and November 1959, November 1960, December 1961 issues)
"At Mrs. R's," "City Park: Spring," "Coming Home," and "Year-Round." Copyright © 1959, 1960, 1961 Constance Hunting.

THIS BOOK PUBLISHED SIMULTANEOUSLY IN
THE UNITED STATES OF AMERICA AND IN CANADA—
COPYRIGHT UNDER THE BERNE CONVENTION

ALL RIGHTS RESERVED. NO PART OF THIS BOOK
MAY BE REPRODUCED IN ANY FORM WITHOUT
THE PERMISSION OF CHARLES SCRIBNER'S SONS.

A—1.69 [c]

PRINTED IN THE UNITED STATES OF AMERICA

LIBRARY OF CONGRESS CATALOG CARD NUMBER 68-57076

CONTENTS

City Park: Spring   1
Bird in Hand   2
Miss Dickinson   3
The Ride   5
Coming Home   6
Concentration   8
Martha Song   9
Beldam   10
On the Possible Killing of a
     Three-Months Child by a Rabbit   11
Transferences   12
Fever   13
Year-Round   14
After the Stravinsky Concert   16
Revenant   20
The Heron   27
Conversation: Late Day   39
The Gathering   43
Afternoon of a Contemporary Poet   54
The Perfectionist   55
At Mrs. R's   57

Morning at the Museum:
    15th Century Collection   59
A Dream of Heavenly Love and
    Redemption in the Wood   61
Musing in New England: The Long
    Last Day of Mrs. Eddicombe   63

AFTER THE STRAVINSKY CONCERT
And Other Poems

CITY PARK: SPRING

On Sunday afternoons the girls
in their thin silk dresses walk out lithe
bellies swaying bottoms swinging
while pince-nez pigeons creak aside
pretending with a superb
unnoticed condescension no acquaintance
but the old benched men
sifting the ashes of yesterday's
newspapers sense behind their eyeballs
distant burning
signals of countries long unvisited
and sailors
stealthily detach themselves from chewing gum
and start the stalk and all the leaves
are green again.

BIRD IN HAND

The way the poet eats the hard-boiled egg
is this: he first chips delicately all round
the thin resistance of the shell of fact
which falls like flakes (if alabaster
melted so it would before
his beaming eye) as flicked
by his dactylic finger, to reveal
the gleaming nacreous shape
like a monstrous pearl—
he bites, good appetite, the simile in two
and sinks his teeth in muse's pollen,
golden, dusty, the real thing
that might once spring a phoenix to confound
the ovoid gape of his astonied stare.

MISS DICKINSON

She cut the wrapping paper neatly
into rectangles—no one would ask why,
it was New England's way—you saved
against the day. No matter what

the parcel had contained,
butcher's delivery, book
by some downstate sage, immediate
scissors flamed in her pocket.

New England makes its women
strange now and then—they take
to cats, or murder, often
in multiples; but she,

compound of thrift and greed
in primstitched white, preferred
to catechize mortality
in the side yard, and afterward

scratched on what leaves
(maple, perhaps, or elm)
only an oracle of Amherst,
Massachusetts, could command

the gist of the matter. Thrift
may have special uses—
likely the household's
other women saved the string.

THE RIDE

The white hair of the old
lady in the closed
window of the black
automobile. She sits
very straight, looking from right
to left as the car
turns the corner.
She is being taken for a ride, is it
by her son or perhaps a dutiful
middle-aged nephew.
The trees drop a few leaves in token.

Ach, the white
cotton wool
and the two grasshopper eyes
peering on stalks this way
and that.
She is helpless, she is old.
I do not want to be like that
taken for a ride by Mr. I-Don't-Know.
Keep your leaves, trees, don't write to me.

COMING HOME

I leave my armor by the umbrella stand and enter.
  At the first word I think of stone
    walls, sea meadows, and the sweet
      fearful smiles of old ladies in streetcars.

Blood of my blood and bone of my bone
they sit and stare me down.
His hands with tender spots of age
spread like soft meat on either knee.
"The hollyhocks this year—the salt air
brightens them, y' know. (Had you forgotten?)
What d' you have out there—
linden, is it? Immigrant shrub."
Her fingers clasp each other in the lap
where once, unborn, I must have leapt
half symbol, half embarrassment.
"We were a little disappointed—" she begins
with terrible timidity.
Love trembles in the proffered cup.
Then seedling, shifting, swelling,
sprouting, flourishing, brandishing, shaking-
shouting tree of pride, fruits pumice-
textured, clustered, shrunken,
color of never and despair—
                but after all,
what have they done to me, what crime

committed time on time in this small room?
And my own children, yet to be?
Splay-fingered, milky-mouthed, they will of course
love me, love me, love me.

CONCENTRATION

Goody-Goody's
thrown on the fire
there she goes
there she is

shovel of ash

Her little toenails
like blackened rose petals

Here is her hatpin
here is her buttonhook
here is her gold tooth
It is a game of objects that we play

MARTHA SONG

I go about my house with a dustcloth every blessed
morning.
Sweep and vac
front to back

shake the mop from upstairs windows
wipe the sills and polish dead
curves of furniture.

What the table what the chair
don't say when I'm not there
I'm sure

I should care. I shine china plates like smiles.
My house gleams
like a shell.

If I remember, if I have the time
I might carry water outside to the dying

flowers I planted in baked cracked earth.
Christ!

BELDAM

Now that I'm certified,
now I'm insane,
I don't have to come in
out of the rain,

I wear the cap and bells,
I bear the drums,
and I won't tell you
when the bogeyman comes.

I go by children
I hold my breath
so it won't fall on,
pearl them with death.

Abba, I nibble on water,
Abba, I moon on air.
Later, I'll show you the mousehole
under the tilted stair.

ON THE POSSIBLE KILLING OF
A THREE-MONTHS CHILD BY A RABBIT

Was it raining, did the street lights bleed
rosy haloes through the city mist?
The weather might be important.
Was it a beautiful night?
Oh, the red eyes, oh, the vibrissa
hanging over the raddled couch.
And the fur, like cotton candy, like the ghost of the
                              biggest
snowman.
Where did it grow, how did it get itself
out of the cage, out of the newspapers?
It was someone's pet, for God's sake?
WHO WAS THE FRIEND?
The father snores.
I knew a lady once pulled out
her eyelashes by the roots.
She was tall as a poplar,
pale as an ash.
Did the flesh
taste sweet, like new lettuce leaves,
wild onions, milky as white rose petals?
From the little stump a rubbery string
drools like the shred
of a red balloon. Sleep, baby.

TRANSFERENCES

This is my year for looking
ironically beautiful.
People respond to me.
What big eyes I have!

They are glass.
Such glossy hair,
it is made of damp chestnut leaves.

My skin has the fashionable
pallor of arsenic.
And that fine-boned nose!
Precisely.

Ego is a malodorous weed.
Such long nails!

FEVER

I take it my real child is ill.
The worm works in the rose, and fever
glisters in tower windows.
Can my thorn draw her poison?
Extreme caution must be exercised.
I must exercise extreme caution.
My medicine is very powerful.
It has already killed several.
I stand at the foot of her white bed
and tell her of her pet toad
whom she has named Mortimer, after
a friend of the family. I say that Mortimer,
patient, self-effacing, utterly reliable,
waits for her under the laurel hedge.
Her eyes are so bright!
Outside, the rain falls like fat gray slugs.

YEAR-ROUND

With what deceptive
gradualness the summer guests
depart,
bearing the various trophies
of their stay, shells, driftwood
antlers, a seabird's skull,
leaving
for our instruction shards
of the season's visit: sand on the stairs,
odd sneakers, a torn sweater, a child's ball,
and on the dressing table an unmailed letter.

One afternoon the last car disappears.
The hand raised in farewell
flags, drops. We linger
a moment at the edge of lawn,
knowing that soon we must go in,
desert the view, diminish
scene. Bring in the chairs
from the terrace, store the picnic things,
cover the boat. The house will need repairs—
look, that shutter
flaps.

Only, the clock
gnaws in the hall
like a mouse in the rind

of yellow time.
Let us make tea, learn chess,
revive the art
of conversation; read; take naps.
A toothless sea
mumbles at the crusts of the land.

AFTER THE STRAVINSKY CONCERT

i

One day the pier glass in the entrance hall
swayed slightly, shuddered, and slid down the wall.
Just so an aunt of mine

Introduzione: was found once, sitting on the parquetry

voce
principale

in the same place near dawn, her wreath awry
and roses on her breath; but that perhaps
is neither here nor there, the glass uniting both
having long since been carried to the lumber-room,
leaving us nothing to reflect upon. The gilded frame
was loosened and the mirror cracked. A cherub lost
a flying ribbon and whatever
had been underneath was only plaster.

ii

Fell of its own weight was the verdict I knew better
girl though I was then not yet risen
from the kitchen where that afternoon
the dishes rattled like the bowels
of a starving man they said along the gallery

*Larghetto
indeciso:*

vocina

the pictures swung as if freshly hanged
and in the drawing-room the vases chattered
like nervous women in a thunderstorm—
it was the boys

old men now stuffed with honors till their eyes
bulge out as if already marble
noble this and noble that on Sundays
glossy in the sups you might have seen
my photo too last birthday toothless I looked
but at least alive—I was saying
the nephews jumping on the beds upstairs
that was the cause. Your grandmother
was fond of them Lord alone knows why fond-
foolish if you ask me or else proud
to be bewildered so.
They should never have been invited at all.

iii

Not half an hour before the fall, my grandmother
had stood impaling with the perfect calm
of confidence in time and place her floating hat
upon a pin; perfectly gentle, perfectly good,
pierced thus the instant, crowned herself
innocent patroness of place and time.
This was her afternoon to call.

dante
tenuto:

:e
ncipale

The mirror gave her back her face
wondrously like: she knew
exactly where she was within the frame,
could lift a gloved finger if she wished
to touch the earlobe where the pearldrop sprung
chaste fruit of gold, and what she saw
she touched could feel, by sense and reason

mirror-assured that touch and sight were one,
aspects of distance and the moment joined
in a grave image of reality, as if she had been swan
and glass the stilled
water she moved on, making a single silvered self
(liable, however, to current and the wind
shaking the silvered surface of the dream).
When she came home, here the great boys had been
and had their game. She did not scold; said merely
she had been fond of it; had it put away.
The frame, she said, might someday be of use.

iv

The house stayed wide, the gardens blowing
garlands of light and roses through the open doors,
the lawns with blandly insolent grace unrolled
in green chiaroscuro to the little lake

Scherzo,
mancando
poco a poco:

voce
principale

below the pavilion where the spoilt peacock screamed
for tidbits from the luncheon guests who strolled
in clothes appropriate to the view.
Beyond, the ground-flowers in the meadows fairly
hiccupped out of the grass, and the gilt-edged sun
beat like a gong about the rooks all summer long
wheeling and wheeling in the burnished sky.
We never saw it that way.
Something had altered by the time we came,
something we could not put a finger on
but felt insensibly the absence of

had been withdrawn; some force which would surround,
protect, make fast a floating present; stay
the nettle and keep out the rot.
The place seemed at loose ends.
When we first found the pier-glass in the lumber-room
we were amused a while to see how true
had cracked so easily to false, or, it might be,
from false to true; and minced and mimed,
though Reba, the youngest, held up, cried:
her nose was flawed like her old doll's.
The game queered, we slammed outside.
The sky was threatening somehow; had crazed,
turned tarnished, and at the last
let down its brittle rain.
We sat against the wall and watched
the season going under in the fall.

v

This is November of no beggars riding,
no more strawberries and cream, when Babylon
Finale:
grave assai: is gone out with the candle and the seam
is none too fine. Night descends early now,
coro it's hard to tell the substance by these shadows.
The thin wind blows hey moaney o,
fragments and shards! fragments and shards!
No nonnies, no nannies, no go, lovely rose.
We sit against the wall and stare
into the splintering of air.

✿✿✿   19

REVENANT

i

The day my father died in burning fall,
pyres were lit all up and down the streets;
and on the afternoon I saw his recent ghost
it came—no more a Lucifer
than any other man's or Faustus either—
it came, again I say, upon the haze
hung like a summer's cerements
thick and sententious in the anxious air.
But he came quick, familiar glint
of calmly humorous inquiry
a nick in the corner of his eye.
Windows were open, I was playing
unaccustomed Chopin in the mist
that smoked the mirror, made the cat cough
and curled the fern's fingers back towards dust.
Had I been playing Bach
I doubt my father would have come,
for, as it happened, he had only one
piece to his name,
almost the slowest Prelude in the book,
single survivor of surly Saturday mornings
chopped into little pieces by the clock
while in his brain the spit-lovely, curving ball
arced purely, maddeningly, through seraphic blue.

Surely the teacher stayed, let alone returned,
solely because of my grandmother's coffee,
deep, strong, and bitterly bracing,
support, so she claimed, for the silver spoon
dipped by the innocent into the red-gold brew
this clattering tall witch brought with the steam
still on it, fresh from her chivvying.
The boy slipped out and ran towards his own way.

I knew the parlor well, from childhood summers on.
Cool, high-ceilinged, rosewood, mahogany,
words over memory like a chime: here shall they sit,
be summoned up and wound, submit once more,
the foreign, patient master with his awkward shoes
primly together under the dark plush pall,
the talking woman with her full blue eyes
flashing out kindness as it were argument.
The table between them's firm as the equator.
Beside these curios, those in the what-not dim
(even the giant conch, borne back a trophy,
pink as a god's other ear, from Atlantic City
and my grandparents' wedding trip).

                                        She lets him off
before he grows too weary, but she does not fail
to note the exhaustion of his drooping cuffs.
It does not matter that I never saw him.
He wore a pince-nez, parted his thin gray hair
in the center, had a trick

of pressing his finger-ends as though in prayer;
lived in one room above the post office,
had no piano, practised at the church;
cared overmuch for beauty considering
his means and his existence; died
weightless, smiling ambiguously, and left no will.
And yet my father learned his piece.

iii

Ontario springs are rain-flogged out of winter's
chilblained grip. Ice boomed
and buckled on the Chippewa, the puck
skidded, striking rime in sprays; girls screamed,
scarves streaming red like February dawns,
as the whip snapped and skirts went flying
showing a tingling glimpse of wrinkled cotton shins.
By late March the ice was used up, yellow,
and willows took the yellow towards their green.
You had to watch the rotted wooden sidewalks
as, burbling with tonic, challenging the cracks,
you swaggered out adolescent as the season.
From the veranda, Emma and Maud waved Saturday
dustcloths and shouted something rude.

They were the older sisters, Allegra next,
Bertha the baby. My father was nearly christened Paul,
indeed was called so for his first few months,
but my grandmother changed her mind the week before

the ceremony; she had no time to read
except while nursing, and that year
it was Goethe (in translation), so it was John
anglicized and wailing in his lace-trimmed robe
who was sprinkled the only son instead.

My grandfather was in groceries,
natural gas, washing machines, lord knows,—
a Personage with a capital,
the cock of his hat, the lilt of his moustache,
the heft of chain across his vest told that.
Raised in the midst of presbyters,
he backslid gradually from divvying
the children with his Anglican
on alternate Sundays to the porch
hammock and counting ruby-throated
hummingbirds while, very black-and-white,
very erect, she set out trailing charges
like a swift silken kite. "Fifty-six
at service," she would report, and he
respond, "Eleven at the trumpet vine."

One day they take the boat to Buffalo,
he has a man to see; she has the stores,
of course, and asks no questions, being here,
and only here, diffident. They arrange to meet
at 2 p.m. at a monument they both like.
She is there. She is there a good hour,
grown very tall, moreover, and beset
by pigeons. "Tommy," she says in a voice

of thinnest glass, "where have you been?"
"I've been flying," says Grandfather, "all over Buffalo
with Sir Harry Oakes in his private plane.
He found it was my birthday." And settles his chin
onto his collar with absolute éclat.
He took five teaspoonsful of sugar in his milk,
but it was Russian rubles did him in at last.

His mother lived along another street.
John was her favorite. A little boy
in knickers with a devilish bright eye
he stood behind her chair in hottest June
and fanned her heaving, purple chest.
Immensely old, immensely fat, she fought
the ostrich feathers with her jagged breath
and wheezed against her fancied ills,
slightings by relatives, stealing by kitchen girls,
asthmatic whispers coiling in his ear
like the fierce distant thunder in a shell.
Still he was fascinated, even when
as it were between complaints she gave a sudden gasp,
clutched at eluding air, and went right under.
It was the silence, not her final glare,
fixed and affronted, freed his howl
and flung the fan down at her slippered feet
and sent him thudding home to beggar noise.
The following week he drowned
Allegra's coral brooch in the sulphur well
and was soundly strapped. His sobs
were loud with gratitude.

Was taught to swim by being rowed
to the river's middle, harnessed to a rope
and tossed in; down he sank
thrashing like any sunny into the rank
muddy whorls, and rose up gagging
for his pa's laughing under his panama;
his father hauled him in hand over hand,
tossed him again, again; until
the boy glistened and panted like a tadpole
and took the other element for pleasure granted.
The sun was staggering on the western slope
when the pronouncement came: "Now you can swim,"
the tamer said, and lit a fresh cigar.
The boy never doubted it was true.
One wet, one dry, they headed for the shore
where Emma flapped the supper semaphore.

iv

A gloss of days: one guesses, one must guess.
In the upstairs hall there hung a length of frame
entitled *Life's High Moments*. After the bassinet,
hooded like a snuffer, and the child
velvet-suited, banged, and guarded by
the Saint Bernard whose tongue lolled sweetly out,
a young gentleman in faultless evening clothes
correctly bowed before a maiden piled with hair.
The next panel showed the wedding, she
impenetrably veiled, and after that

they got into the carriage and were driven off.
And then? And then? We do not know.
We are not apprised. We imagine gone
what we are not sure existed even once—
school fights, bad dreams, the poster pointing
you to fight the Huns: the night the horse was tied
to the banister on the second floor
of Croyden House; free-lance experiments
in foggy fields, knowledge the premised province—
it receded, rather. . . . And all this, all these
gone by and hardly reconciled
with what has come, and been, and gone again.
I enter late,
with other burdens, into smaller rooms.
The dimpled moon that drew you by her smile
into her sphere outlasted you
and now sinks sidewise with her numbing grin
hugely enspreading whatever face you loved.
Can I restore you to a simpler tune
than that which wrangled out our times that mingled
making the players fret and mumble too?
It is dusk now. Do not light the lamp.
Let the place be neutral, somewhere between
my haunted present and your haunting pale.
Peace to the footfall, rapid and sentient;
let be resolved and recognized lost seasons; wait
for the steady, lifeless breathing of the snow.

THE HERON

What does he make of it all,
the solitary blue
heron standing unmoved
and motionless these hours
on the most delicate
elongated leg like black-
lacquered bamboo in the shallows
at the far end of beach beyond
the weedy place where the shore curves
in, against the lake and sky,
and darker and stiller than each?
It is the smaller blue,

not like yet something like
gulls of my childhood, summer's
easy skimmers (how we entered leaping
into the arched hollow murmuring mornings),
divers and swimmers of the foam and air
whose sun warmed the numbed rocks and rose
to be cooled the whole day in the sea,—
stung into alabaster motion by the salt-
spray rush and flash of the glittering roll,
the hugely tremulous coruscating infinite-seeming bolt of blue
drawn out to crash or crawl, to curl along or cover
the lift and sprawl of coast, granite and sands

(we castled, pooled at the water's edge,
and heaped on laughing, quivering-limbed
companion corpses with their heads stuck out
and eyes shut dry on imitation dark,
the resurrection always
miraculously quick, the gritty ritual play of child-
death washed off in the instant's
plunge, the race back
with droplets scattering from our heels, and the gulls'
cries about us like new
flakes of light); free-
wheeling runners of the deep between sky and ocean,

released by season's change from slow-
sailing vessels of dull pewter flight
against the wrinkled slate or purple sullen heave,
or points
of wintry meditation fixed
like puritan heads on pilings sheeted green
with freezing slime for Sunday parents to hold up
to muffled (younger) thumbwise child
sucking with vaporous eyes no more than naughtiness
rewarded in less lenient, February age,—
or was there caught perhaps a latent strange
rich breath from suffering's hoary marshes?—

turned again
transformed forms, their white calls
garlanding granite lovers convolute at noon
in the rude crannied shelter of the rocks'

embrace, come onto just before the jump
in the game's metamorphosis, the circus act
of vaulting miles of lions' backs
humped passive to the flying foot
on their pocked tawny hides: the forced
flailing stop, stumble, tamer spun away
shouting into the spume flung to corroborate
betrayal of beasts thought safe,

and falling, like petals, like wafers dissolving
in the heat's blaze and shimmer, off into gradual silent
sounding while their wings' white phrases
rent in articulating space
wavering,
winding, mending itself without a flaw
over the darkening sea-flayed cliffs, the swaying
sea-buoyed bells off Ninigret,
Sachuest, Quonochontaug and up the bay
to Galilee, Jerusalem on the other side,
chanting in frail monotonous voices borne
on the creaking wind of chasms and islands underneath.

ii

Such paraphernalia trailing,
having already the sight in passing
this morning of the farm wife
crossing the yard to set the fresh-filled basin
for the more timid birds under the mallows hedge,

and a corn-color sun
flowered round as a gold watch in the dome
of a county sky showing fair above the dawn
clouds fraying at the eastern rim, we came
over the slight rise planted in coarse grass
to keep the slope from blowing, this brown sand
grainy as burlap to bare soles. No matter:
there was the lake, and the children streaked
forward to make the first assault on the calm
stretch of tawny beach
like the dozing farm dog one steps over in the entry
almost unnoticing, on the way outdoors
to assume the day
with a flurry of shrieks and splashing, waking the water,
pricking the inland balsam air they know
their shrillness zig-zag echoing
off the bluffs opposite, but the lake
in its level saucer did not tilt even a little bit.
If the heron was here then we did not see him.

iii

Did cocks prepared to split the husk of night
sense alien wing oar steady past the red-
roofed farms and silos sleeping upright
through the dark moving wedge translating dark,
and hesitate so that the sun for once
eluded gaping beaks and sprang
unspurred while doubt turned momentary heads

towards westward wake till memory
or something like for water, reeds,
and a sky caught in a rippled net had curved
him to touch down upon the bordering trees
and shake off flight amid a hood of leaves?

iv

Not till near ten o'clock it must have been,
but out here we are
at least an hour behind, and the day
behind that in summer, so must one go
by appearances, time
out of mind: let us just say

it was after the apparition of the small green boat
from the cove on the lake's further side,
like a pod slid on silk, with the three
figures, faceless, brimmed to scant the glare
and yet delivered by it to a larger sphere,
dowered by mists drawn off, to the shore
watcher shown as they were and something more,
presiders, harbingers, of this clime and that,
ample in faded milkish blue, august in azure paled,
their playing lines like fated threads
to gather up the water-marked
puckered seam of their going, themselves
unmoving, without speech, without haste or lingering
across the middle distance to the reach

of the land's narrow arm escaped,
and glided out of grasp and view of the exterior eye
shuttering to an interval's
suspense like the faint humming of a shell

or a wire rubbed to singing; but not before
the boy and girl made sure of, bobbing oblivious,
and, in the lower corner of the scene,
the shadow sensed of foreign shape or signature
to the event; opening on what old

(parliaments of bent, burnished women
having removed their shoes as for a ceremony
at the tide's turn hauling their flimsy chairs—
wrested from tenement top porches strung with soot-
stippled washing, pickets out
like brawled teeth, staggered by bawling children
obscurely envied from the car
on the short cut home to the cleanly haloing
flame for the kettle and the neuter egg
in the scalded china cup,
with antiseptic lilacs peopling the window screen
above the flat scrubbed table after the Sunday ride
to avoid the indiscriminate humidity—
right into the water for the last look and gossip
while at their feet the new colonial
babies dabbled and tumbled in the rosy foam
and frowning mothers stood in rows, transplanted
caryatids talking of Caesareans by a sea
that was the same yet not the same

as in the former center of the world
now shifted to mere seething in the blood
on pavement Saturday nights in the absence
of eagles for processions; but the old ones sighed
perhaps, hearing the indefatigable gulls scream in
the fishing fleet from a foundered sun)

things wondered at and wound on what loose skein
to brush the thin eyelid of the present
that it interprets instances as signs
or hieroglyphs as presences translating an entire
past into a single form imbued
with color and endowed with breath,

the heron had come forward,
sundering
vines hung charm-like on the doorway
of the cell in the overhanging
wood where light ran tremulous
and vague among tangled roots;
entering
with a soft plosion of elated blue
onto the riffled air, into the clear,
and then the sudden braking by intent
or chance, and the unerring riding down
the invisible flume to the strand,—

but this imagined: what was awaked
aware to was the opaque
countering

by stillness as would not occur
to stone but rather in the pine branch
strict and plumaged, balancing
fluidity and brilliance that would whelm,
blind, drown and drain dry, by a weight
of feathers stitched to finest bone, the oblique answering
to earlier signal quilled in water,
while the children sharply cried their Look!

v

Look! What did his eye,
what does his eye take in
now morning has been swung to afternoon
and we are joined by others of our kind,
now garbled picnics have been spread
and trampled after the Sunday School mass
hazing of the spirit so it thirsts
inordinate for sweet drinks labeled pure
and fresh immersion christens earth's salt innocents?
For still he stands,
not put off by the crowd
or voices multiplying flat syllabic caws
to cause an agitation of the day's sequences
so that the ordering is changed upon the scrim
of intimation as it hangs, gauzy with heat,
before us and we gaze bemused
through drowsy meshes now perturbed

as by insects caucusing above the churned
tepidity towards which he inclines
alert, attentive, strangely courteous
and remote; the grasses trembling slightly
always about him on the littoral. He too must see

how farmers when they get in boats make furrows
out of habit, mariners of the plow,
grins scarring weather-stiffened flesh
at unaccustomed gunwale
antics of their squealing young,
or, at the barrier, how couples with hasped arms
are treading living thigh to thigh,
trading glazed stares and laved
by liquid substitutes, their commerce
languid and the yield foregone; must be
observer of the anxious promenade
of the perpetual second cousin plump and pale
as a puffball, proud no doubt
of her small feet and supple bangled wrists
that tap and toss out vined veranda tunes
on heavy evenings after the faint din-
dunning declension of some dead saint's bells,—
who rigged now in tropic rayon and pink gloves
alarms herself for her dog's sake that the boys
are throwing sand again; again, scans where
shorn of their voyages, shades in the sun
they pushed all day across the prairies,
ravishers of sod and shy of women,
the old men dangling loose in clothes

having more wear than they can use,
the somehow puritan ardor in their veins
turned now to ichor subject to the cold,
watch as from lichened agates how things are
without them as they were, converse
from mossy caverns, hollowly,
halting hawk and spit
rehearsing how the freezing hiss of rheumy rain
plagues the interstices of wind-kilned bones.
But at the first frill of the fretted lake
a child steps and cavorts with a red parasol,
practising earliest deceits and favors
with rosy lady's battered little shadow,
gayest ruins streaming silken ribbons' rivulets.

vi

What shall be made, what shall I make of that? I
who in human guise hover and marvel, spy
and adorer, ruthless pardoner, and find
my mind's eye swells and boggles at such troves,
desiring to embrace the entire, may fail and fall
utterly into my own swift fallacies,
mistaking sight for vision and the naming
for the possession of, likewise the past
for my own simple history (I would not wish
a simple history for anyone),

and either praise too much
or rail how we are islanded in time,
pilgrims and immigrants from a world
we never knew, left languageless,
bereft and half-blind on a rock,
a mere pimple in a vast waste of surly roil,
and turn to picking over bits of broken shell
such as are dropped from indifferent beaks
to smash on granite a sea mile below,—
stooping, we gather up such treasures
slowly, slowly, under the decaying day,
later to lap and mumble in the clammy chambers
who has the most, the prettiest, the best,
and when the night is darker we will murder him,
he having amassed attempted beauty out of litter
and thus a kind of speech and this a crime,—

so fancy runs and blinks and feeds upon the scene
the same yet not the same another eye
assesses opposite: the pinpoint eye,
the glistening black seed of vision, tiny orb
that makes the universe an exercise in minimals,
going back, beyond myth, beyond malignant or benign
interference with earth's dust
molding and naming parts of man,
beyond disappointment then, or shame,
to scale us with the primary essences
we carry in us, equal in value to the pile of sand
before which the boy and girl kneel in attitudes
of curious homage; allowing therefore the return

towards evening to the emptying beach
of actual country women in a small green boat,
a little tired may be and thinking of chores
waiting, and husbands, and certain wicks to trim:
letting them be miraculously what they are.
What do you answer here, my heron? Phoenix
of place, prophetic bird, time's arbiter,
the heron keeps his distance still; and always will.
Voices come flute-like at this hour on the pellucid air.

CONVERSATION: LATE DAY

What was so bright is fading now. Is it not
fading? The sun slants
oddly. *Differently, that's all.*
The paper's peeling roses in the hall.
The boarders use the phone too much, and scratch
their numbers on the wall. I'll move the bench.
But Mr. Quinquagesima will fall
off; he's dead, remember, these two years.
Oh, surely more.
I've given out directions to the girl
to dust around him. I don't want
him disappearing in a cloud like What's-his-name.

Watch your step,
                that brick is crumbling there.
Which frets me. As you know, I don't like change
however small; if this goes on,
earth will be nibbling at my toes.
I could find someone to repair it,
I daresay; I'll ask tomorrow. Don't,
don't speak the word! No, leave it,
since we must learn to give
in, I suppose, to these natural
processes. I sigh; but then to show
I bear no grudge, you may
cut off some heads for me. Over this way,

and with your military cane take care
of that frowziness. I find chrysanthemums
unsatisfactory except as wigs
to scatter thus like pale rinds on the grass.
Grass! It's hay. Where is the boy
who used to come here? Oh, he changed—
changed greatly. . . . Give me your arm:
how firm it is, like a young man's still.
No one would dream
it's sawdust underneath your clothes.
Where is the boy? I beg
you, don't go on
in that direction, you will only
upset yourself. Remember,
we are walking in the garden, and the day
is surely stopped at four o'clock
just as it should be. Is it not?
That shadow has not moved, it has not moved?
I am afraid that sometimes I may sleep
or grow to drowsiness or is it wake?
I know there's something between day and morning
for, though you may laugh, I've felt it there,
a shape between us, not what you may think
but a gray mass, amorphous, breathing
(holding of breath is part of breathing),
biding its time—it's time I hate,
I'll take no notice of it, hear?
Hush, the boarders. One,
the fat girl in pink frosting, hangs
her stockings from the upstairs balcony.

That's only Flossie, of the thick
ankles and thicker mind. *Are you quite fair?*

It's Mrs. Quinquagesima I fear:
she's always praying, on her knees
on the scabby linoleum of her room,
as though through them some transcendental
whisper may yet come. Why does she leave
her door open? When I pass
she's spitting in her palms. Prayer
makes me uneasy. *Incense is bound*
to fester in this air; would it divert you
if we took another turn, as far, say,
as the firebush, or perhaps
the boneyard? Yes, that dog
is getting beyond himself. The pile
sprouts like the tusks of old
potatoes, and I see
the tatting on the roof
of the house is raveling, but then
tatting's susceptible to weather.

Can't you arrange it so one season
will include all? *As it was I had to touch*
the capital, I had to vouch to keep
these gobblers of your grandmother's preserves!
The cellar's deep, the shelves hold what we need.
Remember other suppers waiting, clean
new-laid eggs, rice-chicken-fish on the checkered
cloth; the cook impatient (servants always are)?

But it was summer then. . . . You have distracted me:
where is the sun
now? Terror, I feel terror.
My shawl, hand me my shawl, the chill
will shake me open so I'll spill
like birdseed. *Close your eyes, you must
close your eyes to hoard the light
from day to morning.* Was that bells
beyond the wall, or only thunder?
My hair smells sulphurous. *Come in,
my dearest love, and close your eyes.*
Your chatter maddens me. *I meant
to comfort you.* You meant, you meant—
it's I who means, you're simply cursed
with what I mean and what I've had to do.
Don't dwell on it. Hurry, come in,

I tell you the bush is blackening.
The sky is washed with yellow. How the trees swell,
as though they'd crack like knuckles.
Will you come? Yes, yes, yes, yes,
you are right. We must look
alive.

THE GATHERING

Evening: At Table

I have remembered sense of generations
packing in close about a feast of time
as though existence were a dining table,
we the invited guests, and I a child again
and pressed between the two tall bony aunts
whose silk skirts spill along my skinny shanks,
whose heads like weedy flowers nod
emphatically across me on their stems
showing the stringy tautened cords
attaching them to Sundays such as these.

Summer. Evening. The dark-veined honeycomb
of glass, the colored dome to childish eyes
a marvel is slid downward on its chain
and sheds its colors as it comes
to harlequin us all. Features stand out
suddenly: an older uncle will begin to look
like his own mother as she looked in age;
his wife will give her maiden name away
in her hand's shape, as if a common line
were written in her palm,—
a dozen like it gesture down the row.
Light falls upon a cheek as it did years

ago for someone else,
and little Shelagh's got the double crown.
We pass our plates up for the victuals,
talking the whole time, or the grown people do,—
interspersed others clutch soft silver spoons
teethed over long since by their elders;
eager in bibs, and propped, they lean
forward and breathe, and slobber slightly,
dazed by the noise, the smells, the light.
(A missing few went earlier to bed,
netted about in hasty cots to listen to
the last birds meting out a day
so brief it must have seemed the sun
opened its eye once fully, gazed gold, then
drowsed it closed again with theirs
and let the mottoes fade upon the wall
and vines and roses over them grow fast
in flowing dark, and cover up
their names.)
Outside, the moths beat furious at the window screen.
The lamp above us glows its blood-
red, blue, its brooding green;
but while the voices rise,
I see my mother sitting silent, pale,
skewered to pride and shyness by her cameo.

Evening: The Mother

She sits stiff, crumbling bread, the smile
stretched tight upon her linen face.
Talk tires her, she often says.
Her rages are so private that they've bleached her gaze,
held lowered now lest it should show
dread or revulsion of the human tribe
she's been betrayed to. Oh, she is cold,
she cannot stand the draught
coiling round her shoulder. She is dry,
as though some spring were sealed from birth,
yet she can weep. She can weep.
Children she loves most when they sleep
or are ill; no one is then kinder,
gentler, more solicitous. Children when they sleep
must be covered; must not thrash; when ill
may be cared for tenderly; otherwise
must be punished gravely, else discover sin,
which will result in telling lies.
Stay still, she murmurs in her whitened tone,
lie down now; sleep. And goes a shade
of white out of the dusky room.
The child stares fearful into dark,
not knowing why. I will not know
till later what sleep means to her.

Morning: The Grandmother

Long ago
this morning,
flattening myself
against my spine, I try
the top stair.
It makes no outcry, so I test
the next, and it receives me too.
The third step creaks
loudly; it makes a hole
in silence. I draw my foot back just in time
and wait, but the hall
above gives no sign; sleep
still holds them up there in a milky mist.
And I go on, picking my way,
my passage down
to seven o'clock of a fine
midsummer dawning past its rosy wake
and gone to flower within
the oriole window of the hall below.
I follow
clues: the cloudy cape
cowled on the newel post, daubed gloves
damp on silver tray, wet trail along parquet,
and chestnut-colored odor
curling beneath the kitchen door. Aha!
My father's mother, tall, hawk-

nosed and vigilant, has of course made the grand
first tour of the day.
Of the garden. In her man's
straw hat, and galoshes left
by some unremembered guest, and bearing
the flat wicker basket and the shears just as
sharp as mercy, she has visited
her stations; paused
to weed, to snip, to let in air about the roots;
and now, her apron on, the vases out,
poses at the counter, parrying
snapdragons!
Oh, it's you!
she says, and, Good: you can pit cherries.
But I don't know
how, I whine. She
shows me how my thumb can pop
the pit out neat as an eyeball. Charmed,
I set to work, we set to work.
"Juice makes a cherry," says the woman wisely,
sticking in stalks
pendent with bloom. "I wouldn't give a fig
for a cherry without juice."
We laugh easily together.
Shaping the day between us, our wrists run
with warmth, the quickness, the sweet light.

Noon: The Grandfather

I am a lady now for solitude and green
wavering light at parlor French
long windows sunk in vines.
Armchair grandeur! Splendor of rosewood and mahogany, and don't forget
the faded Turkish carpet on the floor,
the mends don't show.
I pull a book whose leather flakes
like dried leaves from the shelf.
Happens it's Shakespeare, as I like it,
me, myself, some Rosalind
half-boy, all brave new world,
Miranda, root: to be wondered at, and lost
in profound reality, I reel a little, and read on.
"A dreadful light
to see by," says my prosperous
grandfather's voice from the doorway:
fingering the gold
chain across his vest, he makes his choice,
advances to the piano stool, and sits,
knee cocked jaunty over
other, Sabbath trouser leg. Oh, the swell
his prideful belly makes in person and in place.
You'd think he embodied half the globe.
I do not quarrel with that. I admire
his black magic broadcloth and his milkweed hair.

He smells of Yardley's, wears a boutonniere,
he counts
his children's children like his dividends.
He describes a half turn on his axis,
shoots his cuffs and flexes
manicured fingers over the yellowed keys,
that tumble to his touch like dominoes.
Shower of notes, pattern of ivory tune
woven into leaves that tremble each
a listening, veined, lady's lobe to tease.
"D' you know
what tune that is?" he asks, not stopping
playing, and I hazard Sunday-wise,
"A hymn?" He chuckles. "Not a bit of it.
'Old Black Joe,' with variations. . . . Ha!"
Not stopping yet, but softer, "Had a colored
handyman once, name of Teller. Simple-
minded, but a wizard with the hoe.
Teller confused me with God. Got so
your grandmother called me that to him.
'God wants the radishes thinned. God wants
the bay hitched up, He has to see a man.'
One day the tool shed caught fire. Teller yelled,
'Get God and send a bucket!' Shack gutted.
Teller only said God moved too slow."
"And did she ever call you God after that?"
Diminuendo and amused, "You know,"
he says, "she never did."
And musing, slows, bemused,
stops. "Perhaps that was just as well."

His smile is not for me. " 'It is the cause,
my soul. . . .' What was his wife's
name? Daisy. Yes." Light and quick shadow play
across his face. The tall black clock lets fall
eleven wafers into the crack of time.

v

Noon, Afternoon: Relatives

Uncle Johnny comes just then,
dares to ask if that's too soon,
one eye blue and one eye brown,
hand out always, grin turned on,
plunks him down and starts to croon
how his wife has left again.
How I love my uncle John.

Twin
ancients, sisters in their skin
and bone
of bone, but somehow
fleshless in their scrawn,
sit side by side in lady
chairs and bleed disdain.
High thoughts have drawn their tempers thin.
Dried lips are formed to speak
a no, or yawn.
They have forgot, if ever they have known,
how seldom is a goose mistook for swan.

The Beauty

Is there no beauty here? Yes, in she comes,
bearing the rosy garland of her afternoon
that has not yet begun to wane;
pranced after by her two young blooms,
two variants of a single stem
so smooth, so slender as to seem
new-sprung, although the lines
like light thorn-marks have, in the light,
begun to show beneath those beaming eyes
that shed light like twin prodigals of love.
Her husband walks a pace behind.
"Father!" she says, and stoops
to conquer that old bastion with a kiss.
"Now, Eva," he says, skittish, pleased.
"I saw you only yesterday."
And pats her bottom as a fond papa will.
Her husband glares.
He cannot help it that he looks so pale,
as if he lives forever in the shade.

I look at her, and she is like a swan.

Night: At Table

I float on swirling waters, laughter, voices,
I twirl a silver spoon.
My eyes burn, my head throbs with heat and noise,
but that's all right.
But all the faces look alike.
I hear a tune that runs along my brain,
it recapitulates itself and runs a-new.
It turns me in the whirlpool of a yawn.
And, "Time to go!" My father's voice. He
gathers me, almost hauls me up and away
from light, from the light, the rainbow-shed
blossoming, the giant flower that sways
above our table and our day and days.
"Good-night! Good-night!"

        Later,
awake in the electric dark,
I hear the voices underneath the stars,
departing wheels, the calls, "Good-night!"
Footsteps on stealthy stairs.
And later still the faint click of slow heels
from outside, down on the portico
where the original hosts, arm in familiar arm,
pace like forgiving ghosts,
like the ghosts they will become.
Their guests have all gone home.

He throws away the end of his cigar,
and they go in. Gone home.
The house sighs once, and settles.
Out there, trees stir.
Sap rises in me, and I dream.

AFTERNOON OF A CONTEMPORARY POET

The friend who has a gall bladder
phones: the operation to be done
on Saturday. But only look—
the grand piano, suffering what indignities,
is rolling up the walk,
supported by three men. Crack crack
and crack the floor says, terrified.
"Do all floors do this in all houses
where you deliver pianos?"
"No, lady."
My son arrives from school, bearing a few
sad fallen leaves (it has rained since)
which we must enter immediately in
the dictionary. It is quite full already,
but he does not mind that. And out of these
will spin the tenuous free-wheeling web
of image, while from the top
of the refrigerator the Siamese,
vulture-like, brooding on fancied wrongs,
stares like the ultimate metaphor at five o'clock.

THE PERFECTIONIST

with apologies to John Crowe Ransom

She certainly died, though not
of the general human
fever. Of chills
which proved mortal she died,
and the rigor of pride.
In her vacuum she abhorred
Nature. Nature finally scored.
Her refrain:
"Choose. Reject.
Discard. Maintain.
The stars are false,
they've moved again."
See now the tall
and adamantine brow.
Beneath the lids
closed by the unsought mercy
of the living, eyes must be
still stonied by denial. Strict-
boned hands cling to
a wreath long withered.
Therefore in pity at least
let us bring a winter

garland spiky with unforgiving
green, darkly articulate,
the colder the weather
grows more defiant, and more beautiful.

AT MRS. R's

Breaking the surface of the long, umbrageous room,
rising as from the foam of some dry Venus-sea,
exquisite out of the Aubusson, the tea table:

bearing its rosy wreath of cakes and marzipan,
crested with silver urn perched and craftily jointed
like some heraldic creature wrapt from myth
and set to brood on china (Limoges) eggs.

One looks in vain for a mosaic eye.

The diffident sun, a poor relation
bidden at four, limps in pale vestments,
borrowed, down the andante gloom
peopled with cabinets and manners;
takes refuge finally in ambiguities
of shaded glass shielding too-soft breath
of calculated bloom.

Here pity is no more possible than beauty.

Meanwhile the alternate Thursday connoisseur,
approaching with tainted smile the hooded chair,
notes once again how authentic and how rare

the narrow anachronistic foot
suspended in its pliant, pointed case
of dull bronze leather at the end of the relique-
thin leg of her who is curator and core
of this unique collection opened to a select et cetera.

They say she sometimes sucks a ruby like a plum.

MORNING AT THE MUSEUM:
15TH CENTURY COLLECTION

Being a poet, naturally I was stirred
by such a frame of reference for love.
Now, as you pull on that soft, expensive glove

(which might have clothed some bestiary unicorn
fed in a garden on pears and cream,
brought up to nuzzle lady's fingers
and be rewarded by that same slow smile
a little inattentive, as to a child not hers),

after the morning-full of madonnas
lapped with their haloed embryonic concepts
and all with the special blankness of the eye
showing intensity of spiritual concern
or else phlegmatic before such fruit and blossom
dangled as native to the slopes of Heaven:

after the triptychs spread like holy fans
or the stiff skirts of Flemish virgins
gravid with grace or secret self-possession:

after the landscapes' vague suggestive spiraling
to the mere man-made tower or the tree
transformed somewhere along the corkscrew way
by the foreground domination of the maiden's head
turning them neutral on the cliffs of hills:

something of this and how you knot your scarf
of thinnest, most cerulean gauze
so that it frames your almost plumply oval face,
disturbing to the viewer in its calm
assumption of some prize I cannot even guess,
its inward-dwelling gaze, must give me pause.

"If they could speak," you murmured in the gallery,
"what would they say?"
                              Now your lips part again—
O, may the words fly forth each like a dove—

"Shall we have lunch?"
The blue ends softly fall in place.

A DREAM OF HEAVENLY LOVE
AND REDEMPTION IN THE WOOD

Damn her whose image on my nightly eyes
Rises unbidden by my daytime brain,
Damn her, the false nun gliding black on snow
Within the winter wood to find my places out.
No shudder of stricken leaf foretells
Her coming where I cower amid thorns,
But all the birds sit frozen on the boughs.
Tall as a tower comes she down the ride,
Her train of sable fancies in attendance close;
From a sly fold of her dark habit, lies
Hang like a rosary to be told, or little bells
To cast a different death, to tell a different hour.
Her snouted hounds of Grace and Mercy run beside,
Fawning and leaping on their lengths of chain,
And all the birds sit frozen on the boughs.
Nearer they come, the ladies twittering, but she
Stopping them of a sudden with a hand
Raised as in supplication or surmise—
Mass in the thicket, compound of blood and fear,
Signal of tiny beating in the air, the pulse of red
Betraying the human trespass of the wood.
The dogs know now. Loosed at her nod, they do not
        bark
But come on silent as the trees,
No pause, no check, no circling back, but
        straight

To quarry, that stain on black and white,
And silent spring and before any cry
Can struggle from the beating throat
Beneath them, silently devour.
The softest clapping, as of snowflakes shaken
                    from sleeves,
A smile as calm and faceless as the dark
Attend me on my waking into sleep,
And all the birds sit silent on the boughs.

MUSING IN NEW ENGLAND:
THE LONG LAST DAY OF MRS. EDDICOMBE

". . . and stepping from thy Father's house harnessed a golden chariot, and the strong pinions of thy two swans fair and swift, whirring from heaven through mid-sky, have drawn thee towards the dark earth. . . ."

> Sappho: "To Aphrodite"
> translated by J. M. Edmonds

". . . Ah! when the ghost begins to quicken. . . ."
> W. B. Yeats: "The Cold Heaven"

i

That morning opening
her eyes, cold from the sea-
damp night and seeing Day
again so clearly writ across the
curtains, Mrs. Eddicombe,
a lady of these parts, no longer young
(pluckings of dead
gray hair by dawn on the anxious pillow)
and never beautiful, however vain
(an arch of foot, a turn of wrist
were once admired; she married him
but kept the money in her name

had her two sons, and buried him,—
his actual services
were private, causing talk,
benched wit branched village-green
between hawk and spit
having it that he simply disappeared,
blew away, gone to seed at last
in that cliff-hanging garden up there, or,
wraith of a blithe
adventurer, lit out, West maybe,
past Albany: his stone,
stricken with gull-droppings, leans
anyhow in the churchyard, CAPTAIN
the granite legend reads, ay-uh)

speaks on a sudden out of dream-
disordered sleep: *"Is it time?"*
Receives no answer, has expected none,
not knowing what it is she's asked,
and turns her face away from light.
Something she has been doing now for years.
Must struggle up, to stand upon the mat
and get her bearings. For the floor tilts.
And what old man
stares back at her from silt-encrusted glass?

The slow stair rail unwinds
beneath her sliding palm. The landing window
gives upon the sea. If it is fine
weather, the sea is blue,
if not, the sea is gray.
The weather is fine today.
Mrs. Eddicombe is going down.
As she descends,
the sun through native bull's-eye
shoots such an arrow into her back!

That other witch has come.
She always comes
thank-God early, hobbling on her knobs,
bringing up with her village mist,
heaving the gate,
crushing the oyster shells to grit
(her husband beats her when he drinks,
red as a lobster claw). As to pearls,
pshaw! The rusted key
scrapes seven in the lock.
                    In her cave
she slams pots, chips
blue enamel, works in steam,
issues to empty slops
over the cliff, or hang
the dishrag on the lilac bush.
While in the passage, needle's eye,

the mistress, having lost the thread,
searches along the verdigris-
stained wall for traces of a name.

She hooks her father's cloak
down from its peg that sticks
an admonitory finger out
through moss or mold,
and drapes its holey folds
about her bones. Endure,
endure! She has,
she will. Only, she feels the cold
more than she used to do, and the new
throbbing of a wound she thinks is old.

iii

The formality of walking down the path!
Toad under dock
leaf does not stir.
Why should he budge for this tall shade
that scarcely casts a breath?
Her spells have all run out.
He stays securely under warts
and hides his jewel. A critic's stratagem.
The garden seeds itself, and has this time.
A monstrous cabbage like a coarsened rose
blooms in the lily bed, defiant dreams
a king. Salt dreams. She makes her way

among the golden droppings of the sun,
the silver spittle of the snail.
To come to stone
set like a ruined throne at cliff's edge.
Here she sinks
down, fiddles with her fancy's mourning
thoughts, cedars grow close, and wild
birds coolly cry.

iv

Limpet-born to rock
of woman gone like foam
so soon she never was
remembered, that long time ago
a creature opened,
ignorant of whether eye
or mouth or genital,
but heard the ocean in her father's voice.
Ran free in meadows,
built on sand, went with the wind,
came in to cold, and winter's rheum.
Drank smoke from the chimney.
Somewhere in her father's cups
was introduced to rhyme.
Ah! Scribblings in the eaves,
her breath a freezing cloud
(like water struck from stone),
shadows of metaphors
hung soft as bats among the rafters.

Force brought her out with her
tell-tale finger.
Malevolence
sprung from a black umbrella
shook drops of warning in her father's face
and she found the burrs dragged from her hair
and herself in a tumbril
traveling at terrible speed
into exile, pelted
by mildewed gloves and the smell of pomade
and made to learn her catechism: female.
She never got used to that country.
She got out of it as quick as she could.
But some weakness clung,
and on top of that the old man died
of a brain swelling or a cracked heart
she imagined, and saw him unforgiven
sheeted on the tide.
High and dry
in the pale dune grass she spies upon
the young men
alien as earthly
gods with water-dropleted hair
and their girls in beach-head positions
drilling in the sandy hills.
Her body like a hollow shell. Will no-one come?
She swears she will make flutes
of all the blades within her bone-dry reach.
Will no-one come?
Foam sits the ocean like the ghosts of ghosts.

Her hand beats pitted stone.
She lifts her hand against the light
and gazes at it, wondering what leaf
it reminds her of, altered by air
to wafer flesh. It may fall, it may fall.
Her eyes fill, not with tears
but with ice. So many seasons
in one body! That has borne
the weight of bodies, nomad tenants,
hardly received, hardly nourished,
her fault, her flaw, her unnaturals.
Even her heat then was cold.
When her first was born
she moaned for a pencil.
The second was her favorite.
Till two he spoke no word, and then said,
        "Light!"
At three he looked into her eyes
and said, "Black suns!"
She thinks now he was right,
and smiles a smile she does not know.
At five he gave up metaphor
and joined the other at his grub-dirt games.
She gave them up, and left off feeling warm.
Soon they all treated her like glass,
talking round her, through her, breathing rough
when she froze, but never splintered her,
just vanishing like early frost from pane.

The first bred earthworms in another part
of the country, but the second stayed
to invent a telescope that counted dust.
He had the attic room
till he was committed to a lower roost.
She cleared
his room out, sat her down
and wrote his death to life.

                      So it began,
or ended, the long
betrayal, the long withdrawal—she fell
onto words like spears,
pricked herself time on time like spindles.
She bled rose-red ice.
She in her tower,
and that other
in her cave. Their spells did not collide
but they were in cahoots all the same.
Collusion wound like spider's hair
around the moldings, up the stair.
It came and went like the sea-air
under doors. *Women, we are women here,*
it whispered. *We make monsters in dry wombs*
out of the lime we blow from men's dead bones.
Outside, the ocean laughed and muttered
                in his beard.

vi

Did she sleep? Nod off
in the manner of the old?
It is already quite late.
Some wind forked like a snake's
cool tongue out of the pines
touches her through her shawl.
The sea below is purpling now,
shaking itself like the hem
of the dusk's garment. That is beautiful.
This stone is very hard.
She feels as if it holds her down,
as if she has been buried sitting up
and the earth turned inside out.
She has eaten nothing the whole day,
she could die here
for anyone's care! That is the way,
that is the way of the world.
The saddest phrase. She whimpers.
She must go in. Which way is home?
By the owl's cry, she cannot tell.
She stands. Lost, lost! The sun has gone,
the moon is brewing silver from the sea,
and who, and who will have the last word?
Under his leaf, the toad chuckles in his sleep.

That night, she dreams.
She has been fetched out of dark,
brought back, fed like a child
at the kitchen table. Or was that
dreaming, too? She is sure
she cried and bit the spoon.
She is sure she is lying
in her bed, has long since
heard the shells' farewell,
the white wind
die. The sea asserts its hush,
hush. Curtains
bow once and retire. The night stands wide.
Is it mice gnawing she hears,
moss growing phosphorescent on the walls?
Old houses creak and sigh.
She cannot
uncross her hands from her withered breast.
A board, a bone snaps in the hall.
Light grows in dark if it is rotten.
This rot is dry, and light.
She feels her nails lengthen.
Her tongue stretches, labors: bursts.
A stroke of time, all arching anguish,
thrashing, come, she comes,
the most exquisite. . . .

viii

And love, words, love, her eyes
have startled into stone.
Father, forgive.

ix

Incantatory

Come again come
come all forbidden words
stars beauty flowers even love
put off disguises rise to me
press shells upon my eyes
that I may wake to night or dawn
but not this everlasting lidless nooning
breathe breathe rosy breathing lightly roar
against my parched ear that I may
not die as I have been here on my rock
exposed my tongue turned bitter root
that used to ripple out sound delicate with rime
into the time that had always something of morning
now who will comb
such kelped hair
like dried blood so it cannot hear
and such a dead
sea there dies daily hourly direly
oh I am drying in this sun
I watch the unveiled sky for a flight of swans